How To Play
HARMONICA

A Complete Guide
for Absolute Beginners

Ben Parker

Author: Ben Parker

Editor: Alison McNicol

First published in 2013 by Kyle Craig Publishing

This version updated Dec 2014

Text and illustration copyright © 2013 Kyle Craig Publishing

Design and illustration: Julie Anson

Music set by Ben Parker using Sibelius software

ISBN: 978-1-908707-28-4

A CIP record for this book is available from the British Library.

A Kyle Craig Publication
www.kyle-craig.com

Contents

Introduction

Welcome to **How To Play The Harmonica**. The harmonica is definitely one of the most fun instruments to learn and certainly the most portable. Because it can fit easily in your pocket you can carry one with you wherever you go. Something you just can't say about most other instruments.

From the soundtrack of a thousand cowboy films through the blues of the 1950's and into the soul and the folk rock of the 1960's and 1970's, the harmonica has played an important role in musical history as an incredibly simple, yet brilliantly expressive, instrument.

In this book we aim to give you your first simple steps to playing which can act as a basis for a bright future with the instrument. You'll learn how to play songs using three and two note chords before going on to look at the single note techniques used in blues or 'cross harp' playing.

Also included in the book is a step-by-step guide to reading music. Although most established harmonica players will probably tell you being able to read music is not important, we will use it here to help communicate the various methods you need to learn along the way. Once you have these under your belt you will go on to use the harmonica effectively through improvisation and learning through listening.

 **Practice**

Like any skill, playing an instrument takes a lot of practice. Practicing more regularly for shorter lengths of time is more effective than practicing for an hour or so just once a week.

Learning the harmonica may seem easy at first but it is one of the harder instruments to master the true techniques of. Having it with you at all times will be a really big help.

The recommended minimum amount of practice would be around 15-20 minutes 3 to 4 times a week. The ideal amount would be 20 minutes a day, 7 days a week. Maybe set out a plan of your week and work out the best times to fit your practicing around the other things you do. The more your practice can become part of your weekly or daily routine the better.

It is the returning to the instrument that will make your practice time more worthwhile. So remember little and often is better than a lot, less often.

> *Remember,*
> ***little and often***
> *is best!*

About The Harmonica

The harmonica was developed in Austria and Germany in the early part of the 19th century. Known as a *free-reed* instrument, its popularity grew quickly. Its design was inspired by early Japanese instruments which had multiple reeds encased in a rigid frame.

In the 1850's German clockmaker Matthias Hohner began mass producing the instrument. This original instrument was known as the *diatonic* harmonica. *Diatonic* means it covers the notes of one major scale only. It had 10 holes giving you the ability to play 20 notes covering three octaves but only in one key. You would need another harmonica to play in another key. *Hohner* harmonicas are still the most popular harmonicas today.

Matthias Hohner sent some of his first instruments to relatives in America where its popularity grew quickly. The instrument soon found a place amongst the soldiers on both sides during the American Civil War. Even Abraham Lincoln was seen carrying one in his pocket!

Playing techniques of the 'mouth organ' as it was then known, began to develop and significant new approaches were developed in the 1920's. The most notable of these was the *cross harp* or *2nd position method* of playing.

Around the same time, the *chromatic* harmonica was invented. Unlike the *diatonic* harmonica, the *chromatic* harmonica is capable of playing all twelve notes of the chromatic scale and uses a special button to change the reeds used when playing. Most famously used by players such as Larry Adler and Stevie Wonder, the *chromatic* harmonica is a far more complicated instrument to learn.

In this book we'll focus on the diatonic harmonica only. To keep things simple at this stage we'll only be referring to a *diatonic* harmonica in the key of **C** throughout.

Here's what goes on inside a harmonica:

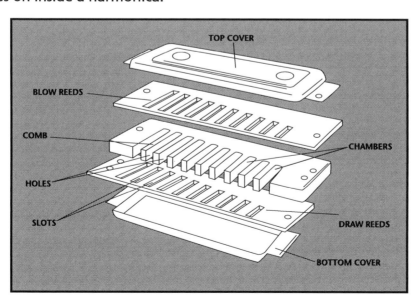

Choosing Your Harmonica

When you go to the music store to buy your first harmonica you may find that you are met with a considerable number of options. The diatonic harmonica is also known as a **harp** — so knowing that will help steer you around the harmonica display case.

The main makes you may see are *Hohner* and *Lee Oskar*. There are other makes which are much cheaper but it is advisable, even at beginners' level, to get a decent instrument. Mainly so you know that any issues you come up against are down to your technique rather than your instrument!

You may see different types of harmonicas by one make such as the Hohner Marine Band and the Hohner Blues Harp. The main differences between these will be what they are made of and their price/quality. Some will have a plastic comb and some will have a wooden comb. Some players prefer plastic, some prefer wood. This is a matter of preference so if you are able to do some research and ask for advice at your music store, you will be able to walk out with the right harmonica for you.

Your diatonic harmonica in the key of **C** should have 10 holes which will be numbered and a large letter '**C**' written somewhere on it.

Hohner Blues Harp and *Hohner Marine Band* with cases.

Harmonica Maintenance

You may think there is very little maintenance necessary with your harmonica but dust can be a big issue so always keep it in its case when you're not playing. Also, try not to play immediately after eating. This may sound odd but you would be amazed what you can transfer from your mouth into your harmonica after dinner! After playing you should gently tap your harmonica against the palm of your hand. This will help to remove any bits of debris that may have stuck in the reeds after playing.

How To Hold Your Harmonica

There are a number of ways to hold a harmonica but the method below is the best place to start. Some people feel more comfortable holding the harmonica in their right hand but see how you go. Try both ways and see which one feels the most comfortable.

Hold your harmonica in your left hand (almost like you were making a sock puppet).

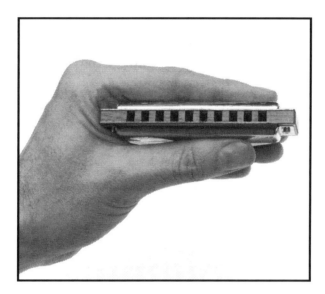

Now bring your right hand up and 'cup' it around your left hand at the end of the harmonica.

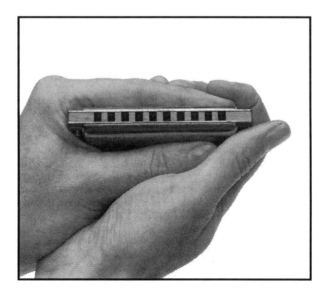

Blowing and 'Drawing'

You are now ready to blow your first notes. Slightly moisten your lips and move them into position as though you were about to blow out a candle. Put the harmonica to your lips and blow into it. You will hear some notes. Notice each hole of the harmonica (numbered 1-10) will make a different note.

Now you have had your first blow you should now try sucking in. We call this *drawing*. We will use this word from now on to talk about sucking in through the harmonica.

With the harmonica to your lips try drawing in air through it. You'll now hear different notes to the ones you heard when blowing.

The harmonica has two sets of reeds. The *blow reeds* on the top and the draw reeds on the bottom. When you blow into the harmonica the air is sent over the *blow reeds* and those particular notes are sounded. When you draw in through the harmonica the air is drawn over the other set of reeds to sound the other range of notes available. This is why, even though you only have 10 holes, you can play up to 20 notes.

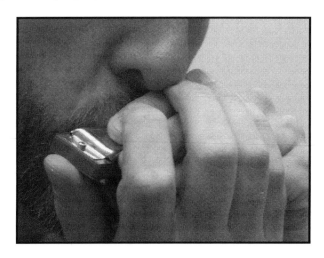

Understanding Music

As mentioned earlier in the book, it is not crucial that you know how to read music but the process of learning will be sped up considerably if you can understand the following:

The notes on the music stave (see below) either sit on the lines or in the spaces. As notes go higher vertically on the stave they go higher in pitch. As they go lower vertically on the stave they go lower in pitch.

Notes in the spaces

Notes on the lines

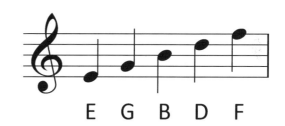

Music runs alphabetically from **A** to **G** and then starts again on **A**. When notes go above or below the stave we use *ledger lines* to keep track of how many spaces/lines down or up they are.

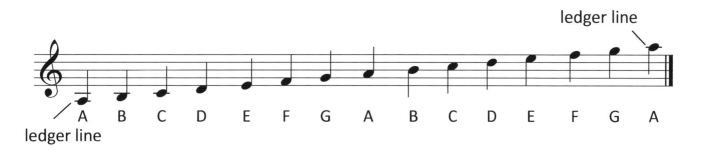

The Notes of Your C Harmonica

Your harmonica's lowest note is **C** and the highest note is two more octaves up. An *octave* is 8 notes ('oct' meaning 8 like 'octopus' or 'octagon'). The journey from the lowest to highest note is called the *range* of the instrument. To show the difference between *blow notes* and *draw notes* the draw note hole numbers are written in circles.

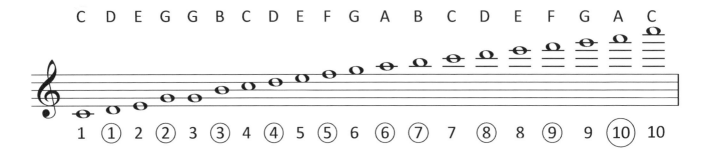

Other Musical Symbols

There are many symbols used in written music. Some are used to help us navigate our way around and some are used to give instructions along the way.

You will see the *Treble Clef* at the beginning of all harmonica music. This tells us where the notes are to be played on the stave.

The *Time Signature* is an important sign at the beginning of any piece of music. It tells us how many beats to count in each bar. At a beginners' level it is only really important to look at the top number. This will tell you how many beats there are in each bar of music.

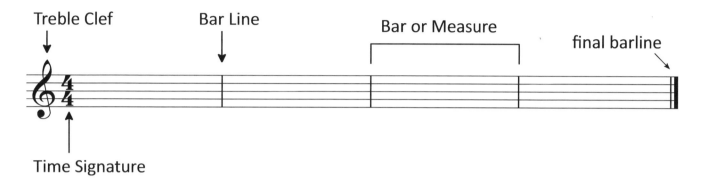

Some notes last for longer than others. To show these different lengths, the notes look different according to their duration.

Notes and Note Lengths

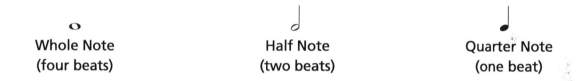

| Whole Note | Half Note | Quarter Note |
| (four beats) | (two beats) | (one beat) |

Repeat Marks

Sometimes you may want to play the same passage of music more than once. To save writing out that passage of music again we use repeat marks. When you see a closing repeat mark you either go back to the opening repeat mark or, if there isn't one, you go back to the beginning of the piece.

Harmonica Tablature

The inclusion of hole numbers with and without circles below harmonica music is known as *tablature.*

To help get the hang of this. Let's try the following exercise. We'll start off by blowing through three holes. You'll see the hole numbers stacked on top of each other to show more than one hole being blown through at the same time. When you play two or more notes at the same time it is known as a *chord.*

> When tablature numbers are show in circles, the note/chord is to be *drawn*.

Remember to hold each chord for 2 beats until the last bar when you hold the chord for 4 whole beats.

Exercise 1

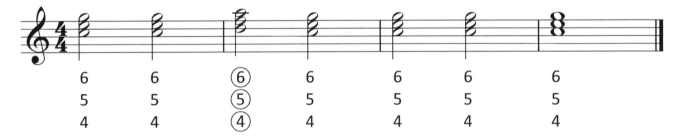

Now try **Exercise 2**. The chords move around a bit more so concentrate on the tab to keep on top of the changes:

Exercise 2

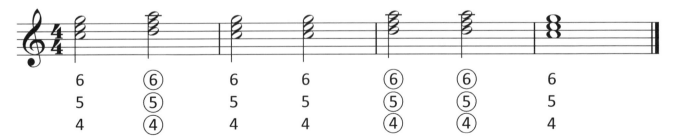

Now you've got the hang of reading the tablature let's try moving down the harmonica rather than blowing and drawing through the same holes. This next tune also has a mixture of quarter notes, half notes and whole notes so make sure you count each bar carefully.

Closing Time

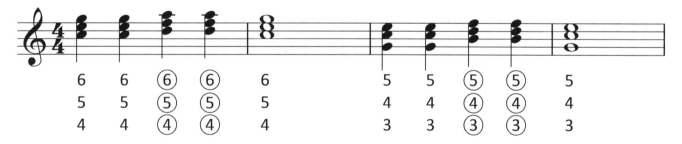

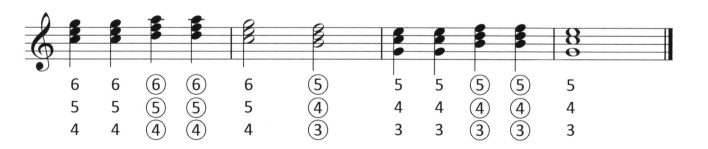

Tonguing

To be able to play more precise rhythms we use the *tonguing* technique. To help explain this, let's imagine we are whispering the word 'too' into the hole/holes of the harmonica. Before blowing, start with your tongue touching the back of your top row of front teeth. As you blow into the harmonica pull your tongue away from the teeth. You can then use the tongue to stop the notes by bringing it back to position behind the front teeth. This process also works when drawing notes. Tonguing will give you far more rhythmic control and is essential for a clear playing technique. Try tonguing **'Closing Time'** on **page 13** to get a feel for it.

Eighth Notes/Quavers

As the pieces you play develop in style and ability you will start to come across *eighth notes*. These last for half a beat. When counting eighth notes use 1 & 2 & 3 & 4 &. This will help you with the rhythm.

Try the exercises below to help you get used to these faster chords. Tonguing the chords will also help you mark their rhythm more clearly.

Eighth Note Exercise 1

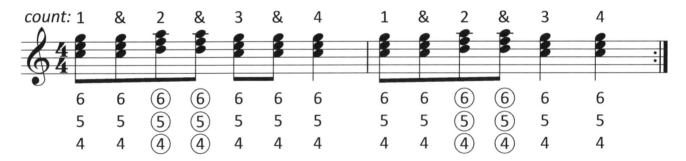

Eighth Note Exercise 2

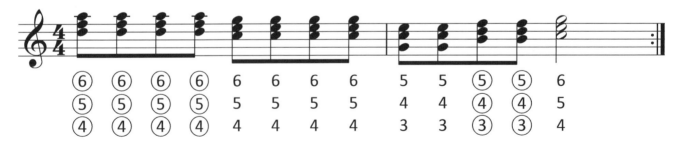

Now let's try **'Frère Jacques'**. Take it slow to begin with so you can get used to the faster eighth note movement in the 3rd line.

Frère Jacques

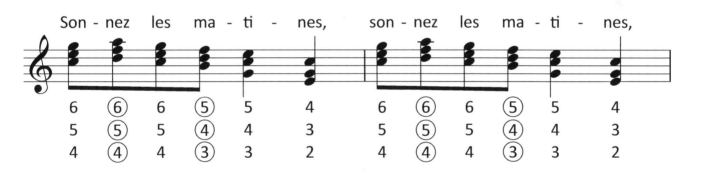

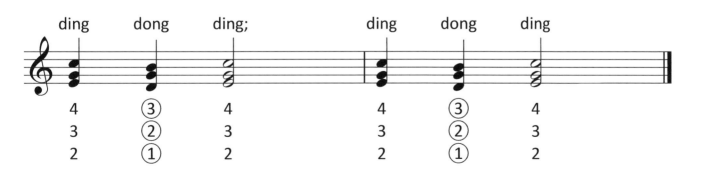

 # Rests

Rests tell us when not to play. Like notes, they last for different lengths of time. This can be quite helpful for breathing when playing the harmonica. These different lengths are shown as different symbols:

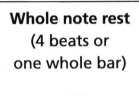

Whole note rest (4 beats or one whole bar)	Half note rest (2 beats)	Quarter note rest (1 beat)	Eighth note rest ($\frac{1}{2}$ beat)

Rest Exercise 1

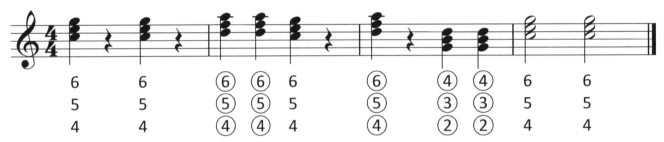

6		6		⑥	⑥	6		⑥		④	④	6		6
5		5		⑤	⑤	5		⑤		③	③	5		5
4		4		④	④	4		④		②	②	4		4

Rest Exercise 2

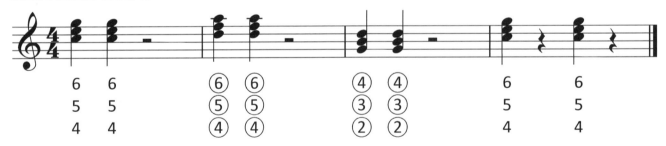

6	6		⑥	⑥		④	④		6	6
5	5		⑤	⑤		③	③		5	5
4	4		④	④		②	②		4	4

Rest Exercise 3

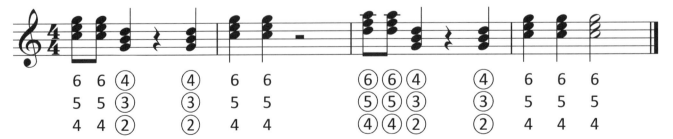

6	6	④		④	6	6		⑥	⑥	④		④	6	6	6
5	5	③		③	5	5		⑤	⑤	③		③	5	5	5
4	4	②		②	4	4		④	④	②		②	4	4	4

Notes with a dot next to them are extended in length by a half of their existing duration. So the dotted half notes in the 'Oh When The Saints' last for 3 beats. Rests can also be dotted too. Also, watch out for the two note chord at the end of line 4. You also have a pick-up bar at the beginning which only has three beats. Also, notice the last bar only has 1 beat to make up for this irregular bar.

Oh When The Saints

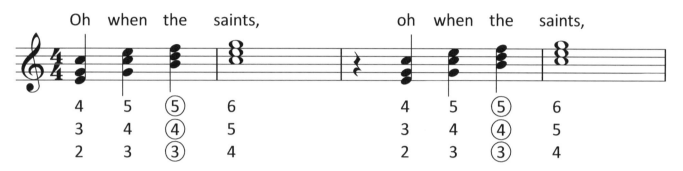

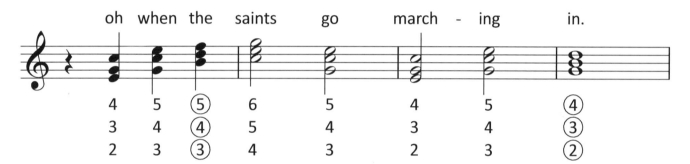

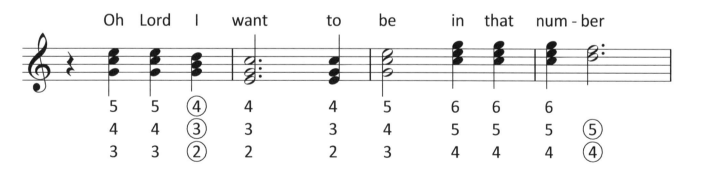

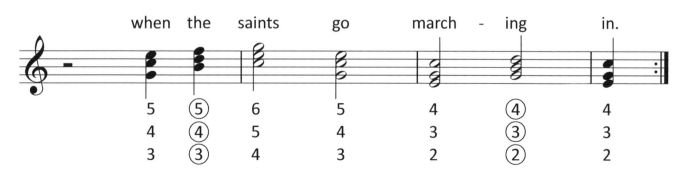

Two Note Chords

Now you have tried mixing your three-note and two-note chords in **'Oh When The Saints'** let's move on to playing a whole piece with just two notes. You'll find the more you play the more precise you can be at choosing which holes and how many to blow and draw through.

Try the following exercises and concentrate on only using the two holes shown in the tablature. It might be tricky at first, especially as you move up and down the harmonica but enough practice and you'll soon find yourself accurately playing just two notes.

Notice they all have repeat marks at the end. Try playing them twice through each time. This will help you work on your breathing.

Two Note Chord Exercise 1

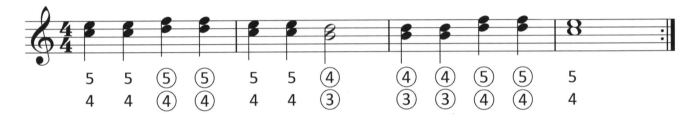

Two Note Chord Exercise 2

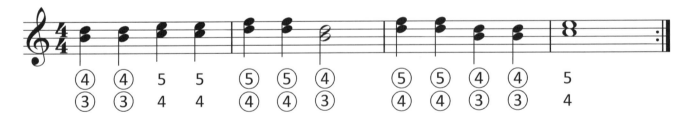

Two Note Chord Exercise 3

Now you have mastered your two-note chord playing, try using this new technique to play **'Jingle Bells'** below. Watch out for the dotted quarter notes in the second and fourth lines. Along with the following eighth note they make a nice 'skip' in the rhythm.

Jingle Bells

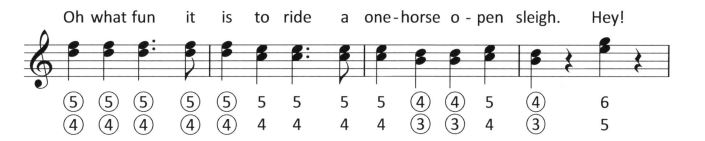

In 'Camptown Races' you'll play a mixture of two-note and three-note chords. You can use the bigger chords to great effect in certain sections of songs where you need a thicker sound.

Camptown Races

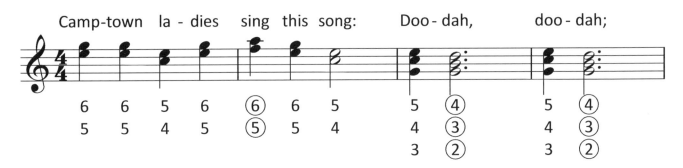

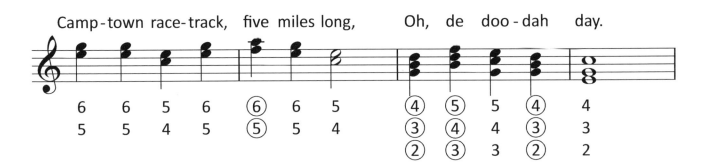

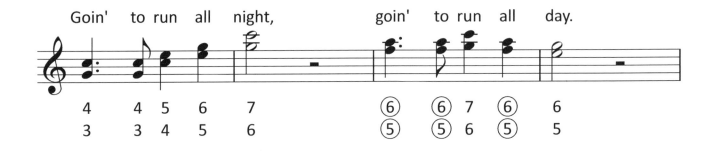

3/4 or 'Waltz' Time

So far all of our pieces and exercises have been written with 4 beats to a bar. 4/4 is probably the most common time signature you will come across. The other time signature you will see a lot is 3/4 (three beats in a bar). Commonly known as **Waltz time** it was also a popular dance in the late 18th century. Try **'Oh, My Darling Clementine'** which is in waltz time.

Oh, My Darling Clementine

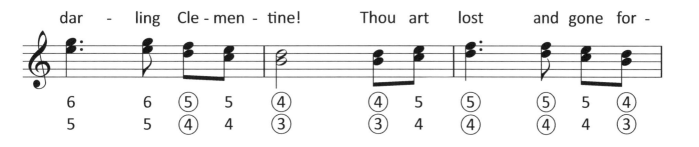

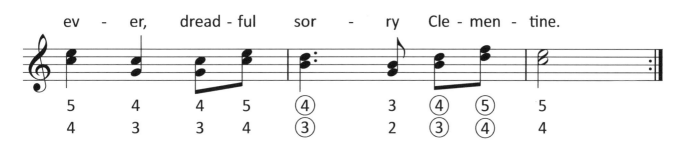

Single Note Playing

So far we have covered two and three note chord playing but our real aim is to develop our technique so we can play single notes. It is much harder to aim your channel of air into — or out through — one hole, but with a lot of practice and concentration and a slight change in approach you can be blowing single note tunes in no time.

First of all you need to try and purse your lips so the hole you are blowing or drawing in through is around same the size as a hole on your harmonica.

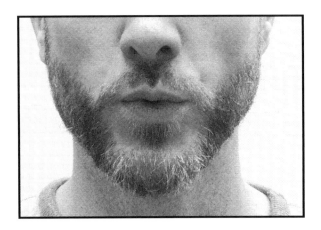

How to work out which note you need

At first you may find it hard to get your aim right with your new 'pursed lips' approach. To hear the note you need clearly you can use your thumbs to cover the surrounding holes to do a test blow or draw before playing the note properly.

Say you are aiming for hole number 3. Use your left hand thumb to cover holes 1 and 2 to the left of hole 3 (photo 1). Then bring your right hand thumb up and cover holes 4, 5 and 6 to the right of hole 3 (photo 2).

Photo 1

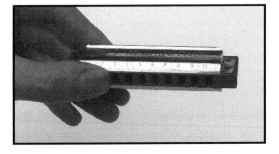

Photo 2

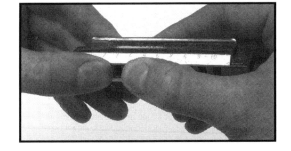

With your thumbs in place you can now blow or draw to hear that one note in isolation.

Single Note Exercises

To get you started with single notes try playing the following exercises. If you have trouble finding your notes use your thumbs as shown on **page 22** to find the right pitches before playing. Remember to blow gently. This will help you aim for each single note and keep the pitch steady.

Single Note Exercise 1

Single Note Exercise 2

Single Note Exercise 3

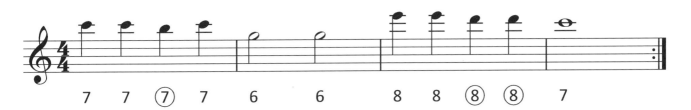

Single Note Exercise 4

Twinkle Twinkle

4   4   6   6   ⑥   ⑥   6   ⑤   ⑤   5   5   ④   ④   4

6   6   ⑤   ⑤   5   5   ④   6   6   ⑤   ⑤   5   5   ④

4   4   6   6   ⑥   ⑥   6   ⑤   ⑤   5   5   ④   ④   4

Long Notes and Ties

Long notes such as the whole note and the half note are often harder to play for beginners. This is because you have to count the beats carefully as you wait for your longer notes to ring on.

A *tie* joins two notes together — you only have to play the first note but it now lasts longer (its length + the length of the note it is tied to).

Try playing **'River Song'** below. Remember to count as you go and watch out for your longer notes at the end of each line.

River Song

Look out for the tied note at the end of **'Silent Night'** — you hold this for 6 whole beats in total.

Silent Night

Oh Susanna

4　④　5　6　6　⑥　6　5　4　④　5　5　④　4

④　4　④　5　6　6　⑥　6　5　4　④

5　5　④　④　4　⑤　⑤　⑥　⑥　⑥

6　6　5　4　④　4　④　5　6　6　⑥

6　5　4　④　5　5　④　④　4

Skip To My Lou

5   5   4   4   5   5 5 6   ④ ④ ③ ③   ④ ④ ④ ⑤

5   5   4   4   5   5 5 6   ④ 5 ⑤ 5   ④   4   4

5   4   5   5 5 6   ④   ③   ④ ④ ④ ⑤

5   4   5   5 5 6   ④ 5 ⑤ 5   ④   4   4

More Complicated Rhythms and Higher Notes

'**She'll Be Coming Round The Mountain**' is a classic harmonica tune. Watch out for the dotted eighth notes and the sixteenth notes. These give the '*round the*' lyric its well-known bounce. You will also cover the 8th and 9th hole notes in this piece

She'll Be Coming Round The Mountain

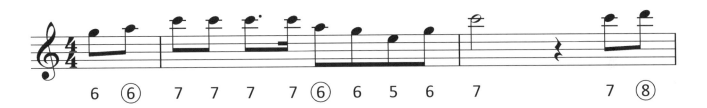

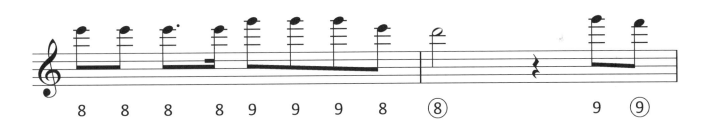

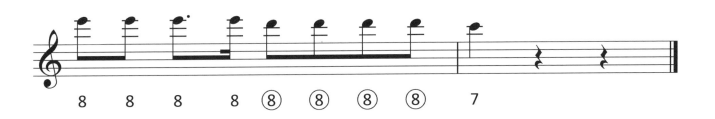

Bending The Notes and Playing The Blues

Now we have learned to play single note tunes we can start to look at *bending*.

In the 1930's and 1940's the harmonica began to establish itself as a blues instrument. In the 1950's famous players such as **Sonny Boy Williamson, Little Walter** and **Howlin' Wolf** would take the instrument and its techniques to the next level. The most important discovery was that the reeds of a harmonica could be manipulated so the notes could be **bent**. This technique had already been established by the great blues guitar players of the era but it was a relatively new concept for the harmonica player.

We know that you can use *blowing* and *drawing* to sound the 20 notes of a diatonic harmonica but these bluesmen discovered that if you change the way you draw (and blow) the air through the instrument you can get the notes to change pitch. It was the sound of the bending notes which has become synonymous with blues harmonica.

How To Bend Your Notes

It is extremely hard to explain how to bend a harmonica note. The most important thing is that the player can really imagine hearing the note bend. This imagination will really help the technique develop. Before you try with your harmonica, try bending your notes as you whistle. The technique is similar.

- First of all, start with a draw note on the 4th hole — in our case, with a **C** harmonica, this note is a **D**

- Draw in through the harmonica as normal with your tongue touching your lower front teeth

- As you draw in imagine the air moving up towards the roof of your mouth

- Now try bringing your tongue down, away from your teeth towards the bottom of your mouth, as though you were changing the pitch of your whistle

- Whilst doing this imagine your tongue movement is pulling the air downwards to form a smaller 'tube' of air

It may take quite a few attempts to start hearing the pitch of the note change. Do stick with it and keep trying. Also, listen to some blues harmonica playing so you can really hear what a bent note sounds like.

The diagrams below should help to show you what your tongue should be doing when bending the note **C** (4th hole draw) down to **C#**.

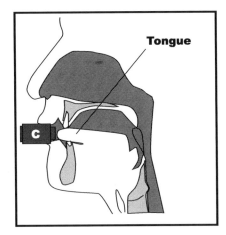

Normal position before drawing

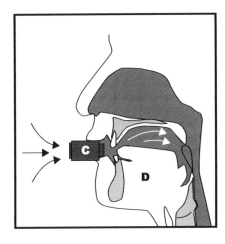

Draw in through hole 4 to sound the D note

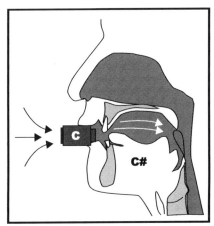

Bring your tongue down, channeling the air downwards

Which Notes To Bend

It is not just the **D** note drawn through the 4th hole that can be bent.

Below is a diagram showing you all the possible bend notes. Eventually you will be able to bend more than a half tone but at this level you'll mainly be looking at the pitches shown.

The blow bends through holes 8, 9 and 10 will be especially tricky to begin with.

Try the draw bends around holes 2, 3 and 4 first. Once you have the technique these will be your go-to bend notes to start with.

This diagram shows the notes for a **C** harmonica only.

Half tone blow bends								E♭	F#	B
Blow notes	**C**	**E**	**G**	**C**	**E**	**G**	**C**	**E**	**G**	**C**
HARMONICA HOLES	**1**	**2**	**3**	**4**	**5**	**6**	**7**	**8**	**9**	**10**
Draw notes	**D**	**G**	**B**	**D**	**F**	**A**	**B**	**D**	**F**	**A**
Half tone draw bends	**C#**	**F#**	**B♭**	**C#**		**A♭**				

Riffs

As you start to play bent notes you'll want to add them to short musical phrases. These are called riffs. The more riffs you learn, the more interesting your blues playing will become.

You'll be shown the bent notes with an arrow coming down from the draw hole note in a circle. We'll look at draw bends only to get you started.

When you play a note then bend it, the two notes will be slurred. A slur shows you 2 or more notes that use the same draw breath. The bent notes will be shown with a flat sign ♭ before them. So a **D** will be bent down to a **D**♭, a **B** will be bent down to an **B**♭ etc. To show a normal **C** or **F** again after it has been sharpened you will see a natural sign ♮. This tells us to play the normal note **C** or **F**. In Tablature, the bent notes are shown with an arrow coming away from the hole number in the direction of the bend.

Some Riffs To Get You Started

Riff 1

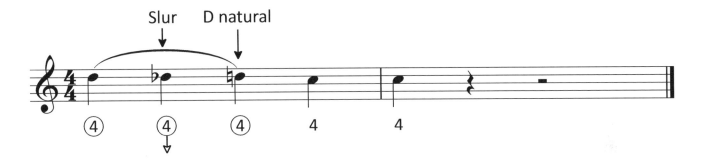

Riff 2

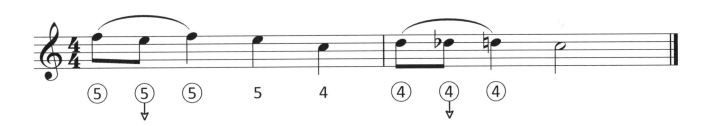

Riff 3

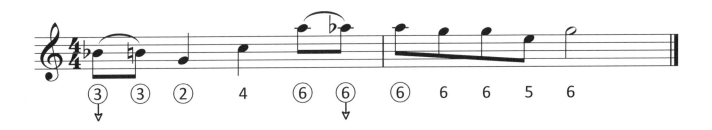

Vibrato/Wah-Wah Effects

Another trick developed by the blues players in the 1940's is the *vibrato* or *wah-wah* effect. This sound can be achieved a number of ways. Firstly let's look at *throat vibrat*o.

Throat Vibrato

This is achieved by quickly moving your tongue backwards and forward in your mouth as you play your note. The tongue movement should be subtle — the aim is to keep the air flowing but to make slight alterations in the channel of air so the note 'shakes'.

Hand Vibrato

You can also achieve the vibrato effect by using your cupped hands as a sound box that you can open and close. Start by holding your harmonica as normal but bring your right hand fingers up to 'cup' the left hand fingers holding the harmonica.

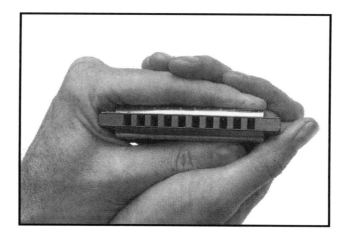

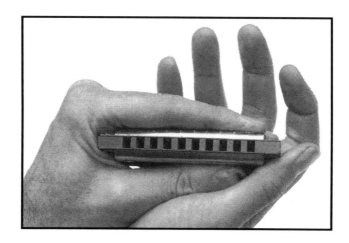

Now try using your vibrato effect when you play **'Streets Of Laredo'**.

Streets Of Laredo

With the bending and vibrato techniques under your belt try combining the two. Here are some more riffs for you to practice with. Long notes will always benefit from vibrato so look out for your whole notes and half notes and try them with a bit of vibrato. Also experiment with a mixture of throat and hand vibrato to see which one works for you.

The following riffs also have some 'pushed' rhythms and some double-note bends. You should try to develop your own style with these. They make that lovely bluesy 'train coming' sound and should be played around with.

More Riffs 1

More Riffs 2

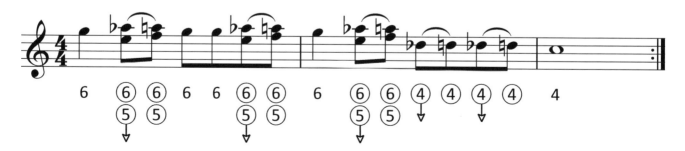

Cross Harp

The more involved you become with playing the harmonica the more you'll start hearing about the **cross harp** technique. **Cross Harp** is also known as the 2nd position technique because the new root note for the harmonica key is played by drawing in through the 2nd hole. Your **C** key harmonica is now a **G** cross harp. Confused? Well, it's about the pattern of notes the harmonica can play when starting from a different key note.

Try the following piece and imagine your **G** note as your new root (or home) note. Because of the new scale available when playing like this you'll get a much bluesier flavour to your melodies.

When playing in the key of **C** your three main chords are **C**, **F** and **G**. Now we're using the cross harp technique our main chords are **G**, **C** and **D**. To help you see where the chords change they will be written above the harmonica stave. For example:

Cross Harp Workout

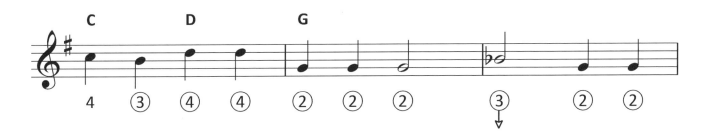

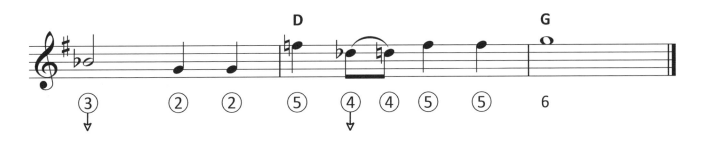

'**Smoke House**' is based on the traditional 12-Bar blues sequence of chords. If you have a friend who could play the chords for you on a guitar or piano you'll really be able to hear how the cross-harp technique transforms the way the notes sound.

Smoke House

Below in **'Rattlesnake Blues'** your vibrato shakes have been written in as wavy lines. These are on bent notes so you'll be better off using the cupped hand technique for this.

Rattlesnake Blues

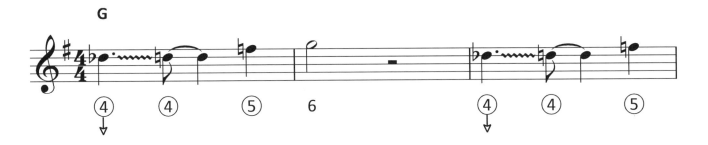

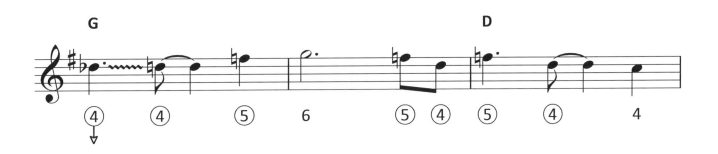

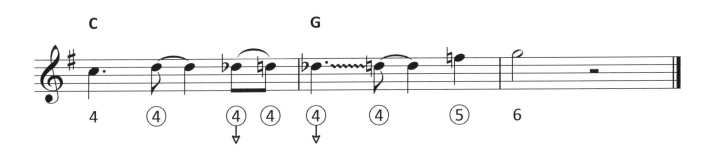

MORE GREAT MUSIC BOOKS FROM KYLE CRAIG!

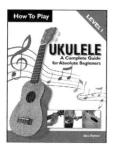

How To Play UKULELE — A Complete Guide for Absolute Beginners

978-1-908-707-08-6

My First UKULELE — Learn to Play: Kids

978-1-908-707-11-6

Easy UKULELE Tunes

978-1-908707-37-6

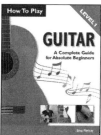

How To Play GUITAR — A Complete Guide for Absolute Beginners

978-1-908-707-09-3

My First GUITAR — Learn to Play: Kids

978-1-908-707-13-0

Easy GUITAR Tunes

978-1-908707-34-5

How To Play KEYBOARD — A Complete Guide for Absolute Beginners

978-1-908-707-14-7

My First KEYBOARD — Learn to Play: Kids

978-1-908-707-15-4

Easy KEYBOARD Tunes

978-1-908707-35-2

How To Play PIANO — A Complete Guide for Absolute Beginners

978-1-908-707-16-1

My First PIANO — Learn to Play: Kids

978-1-908-707-17-8

Easy PIANO Tunes

978-1-908707-33-8

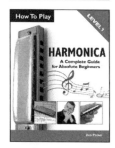

How To Play HARMONICA — A Complete Guide for Absolute Beginners

978-1-908-707-28-4

My First RECORDER — Learn to Play: Kids

978-1-908-707-18-5

Easy RECORDER Tunes

978-1-908707-36-9

How To Play BANJO — A Complete Guide for Absolute Beginners

978-1-908-707-19-2

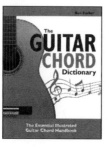

The GUITAR Chord Dictionary

978-1-908707-39-0

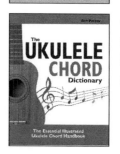

The UKULELE Chord Dictionary

978-1-908707-38-3

Printed in Great Britain
by Amazon

Initial Stage

CW00675774

Ukulele Playing

Compiled by

RGT®

Registry of Guitar Tutors

www.RGT.org

Printed and bound in Great Britain

A CIP record for this publication is available from the British Library
ISBN: 978-1-905908-49-3

Published by Registry Publications

Registry Mews, Wilton Rd, Bexhill, Sussex, TN40 1HY

Text, all musical compositions and arrangements by Tony Skinner.
Music typesetting, additional text and editing by Merv Young.
Design and photography by JAK Images.

Compiled for

Registry of Guitar Tutors
www.RGT.org

v.20140806

Contents

CD track listing

Introduction

This handbook is part of a progressive series of handbooks primarily intended for candidates considering taking a Registry Of Guitar Tutors (RGT) exam in ukulele playing. However, the series also provides a solid foundation of musical education for any ukulele student – whether intending to take an exam or not.

The RGT exams recognise the fact that some ukulele players focus on the ukulele wholly in terms of its role as a chordal/rhythm playing instrument, while other ukulele players prefer to also explore the melody playing potential of the instrument. Consequently, the syllabus structure has been designed so that it can be utilised with equal success by candidates who are developing both melody and rhythm playing skills, as well as by those candidates who are focusing solely on chordal/rhythm playing techniques.

TUNING

This exam is designed for Soprano (a.k.a 'standard'), Concert and Tenor ukulele players that use standard G C E A tuning.

The use of an electronic tuner or other tuning aid, prior to, or at the start of the exam, is permitted.

FRETBOXES

Fretboxes are used to illustrate the chords required at this level.

Vertical lines represent the strings – with the line furthest to the right representing the high A string. Horizontal lines represent the frets.

The numbers on the lines show the recommended fingering: 1 represents the index finger; 2 = the long middle finger; 3 = the ring finger; 4 = the little finger.

0 above a string line indicates that an open (unfretted) string should be played.

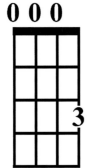

This example means you should press with the third finger at the third fret on the A string; the other strings should be played open.

FINGERING OPTIONS

Throughout the exam, it is entirely the candidate's choice as to whether a pick (plectrum) or fingers or a combination of both are used to strum/pick the strings.

The fret-hand fingerings that are shown in this handbook are those that are most likely to be effective for the widest range of players at this level. However, there are a variety of alternative fingerings that could be used, and any that produce an effective musical result will be acceptable; there is no requirement to use the exact fingerings shown within this handbook.

MELODY NOTATION

Melodies are notated using both traditional musical notation and tablature. Each method of notation is explained below:

Tablature:

Horizontal lines represent the strings (with the top line being the high A string). The numbers on the string lines refer to the frets. 0 on a line means play that string open (unfretted).

The example below means play at the third fret on the A string.

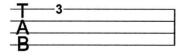

Musical Notation:

Each line, and space between lines, represents a different note. Leger lines are used to extend the stave for low or high notes.

The range of notes that occurs in the melodies at this level is shown below, and included with them here are their string and fret numbers. (Fret-hand fingering is shown with the numbers 1 2 3 4, with 0 indicating an open string; string numbers are shown in a circle.)

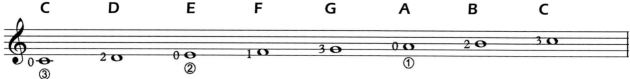

The note names, fingering and string numbers shown above are not included in any of the melodies notated in this handbook. This is to ensure that the music does not become too cluttered, and also to allow for varying approaches in fingering and to encourage music reading.

CHORD SYMBOLS

This handbook (and exam) use the following standard abbreviations when referring to chords:

• The symbol for a major chord is the capital letter of the name of the chord. For example, the symbol for C major is **C** and the symbol for G major is **G**.

• The symbol for a minor chord is the capital letter of the name of the chord plus lower case m. So the symbol for A minor is **Am**.

EXAM TYPES & FORMAT

RGT offers two types of exam for individual ukulele candidates: **Grade Exams** (this handbook covers the material required for the Initial Stage Grade Exam) and **Performance Awards** (this handbook covers the material required for the Initial Level Performance Award).

The Initial Stage Grade Exam contains the following sections:

- Section 1: Rhythm Study

- Section 2: Performance

- Section 3: Free Choice Specialism

- Section 4: Prepared Accompaniment

- Section 5: Musicianship

A maximum of 20 marks may be awarded for each section.

The Initial Level Performance Award does not include the Musicianship section, but instead focuses on performance by requiring two pieces (rather than one as in the grade exam) to be played during the Free Choice Specialism section. The remainder of the requirements for the Initial Level Performance Award are exactly the same as those for the Initial Stage Grade Exam. In the Performance Award a maximum of 20 marks may be awarded for each piece performed.

Grade exams are traditional 'live' exams, where the candidate attends an exam venue at an allotted time and date. However, with Performance Awards three options are available. These are described overleaf.

1. **_Live Performance Award:_** the candidate attends an exam venue and performs their pieces.

2. **_Filmed Performance Award:_** this follows the same format as a Live Performance Award, except that the candidate submits a video recording of their performances rather than attending an exam venue. The video may be submitted on DVD or uploaded via the RGT website. A slightly higher standard of performance will be expected than for a Live Performance Award.

3. **_Recorded Performance Award:_** this follows the same format as a Live Performance Award, except that the candidate submits an audio recording of their performances rather than attending an exam venue. The recording may be submitted on CD or uploaded via the RGT website. A significantly higher standard of performance will be expected than for a Live Performance Award.

Performance Awards are designed for those who prefer to focus on performing pieces. The Filmed and Recorded Performance Awards are also particularly useful for those who find it hard to take time off for an exam or to travel to an exam venue, or for those who get overly nervous in an exam situation, as performances can be submitted by disc or uploaded online without the need to attend an exam venue.

In addition to exams for individuals, RGT also offers ensemble exams for ukulele. For more details see the RGT website www.RGT.org

EXAM ENTRY

Initial Stage Grade Exam:
An exam entry form is provided at the rear of this handbook. This is the only valid entry form for the RGT ukulele Initial Stage grade exam.

Please note that if the entry form is detached and lost, it will not be replaced under any circumstances and the candidate will be required to obtain a replacement handbook to obtain another entry form.

The entry form includes a unique entry code to enable you to enter online via the RGT website www.RGT.org

Initial Level Performance Award:
The entry form and further information about Performance Awards can be downloaded from the RGT website www.RGT.org

Rhythm Study

You should select and play <u>ONE</u> of the four Rhythm Studies from this chapter, using the notated strum pattern.

Performances do not need to be from memory: the handbook may be used during this section of the exam. Remember to bring your handbook to the exam if you do not intend to play from memory; photocopies will not be permitted.

• Each Rhythm Study consists of an 8-bar chord progression in $^4_4$ time that should be played twice before ending on the key chord. (The two sets of vertical dots at the start of bar 1 and at the end of bar 8 indicate the section to be repeated.)

• The notated strum pattern should be played throughout, including during the repeat section – the only exception being that the final closing bar (after the repeat section) should be played with just a single strum rather than with the notated rhythm.

• Either a pick (plectrum) or fingers, or a combination of both, can be used to strum the strings – it is your choice. You should also decide whether to use all downstrokes or a combination of downstrokes and upstrokes – either method is acceptable providing an effective musical result is achieved.

• Tempo indications are for general guidance – performances at slightly slower or faster tempos will be acceptable.

CHORDS

The chords that occur in the Rhythm Studies at this level are: C F G Am

Fretboxes showing the recommended fingering for these chords are provided below:

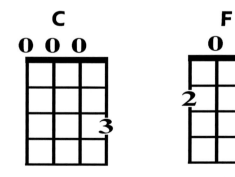
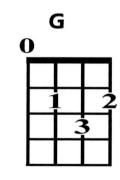
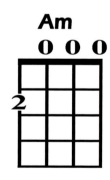

You are not required to use the same chord shape fingerings that are shown here; alternative, musically effective, chord fingerings will be acceptable provided that the chord itself is technically accurate.

RHYTHM STUDY NO. 1

♩ = c80

| ¾ : C | Am | C | Am | |

| F | F | Am | G :| C | ‖

Strum pattern:

♩ ♩ ♩ ♩

This Rhythm Study is in ⁴⁄₄ time – meaning that there are four main beats per bar. The notated strum pattern indicates that you should play on each one of the four beats: 1 2 3 4

LISTEN AND LEARN: Rhythm Study No. 1 can be heard on CD track 1

RHYTHM STUDY NO. 2

♩ = c72

| ¾ : Am | G | Am | G | |

| F | C | G | G :| Am | ‖

Strum pattern:

◇ ♩ ♩

The notated strum pattern indicates that you should play on beats 1, 3 and 4, with the strum on beat 1 left ringing on for two beats : 1 (2) 3 4

LISTEN AND LEARN: Rhythm Study No. 2 can be heard on CD track 2

RHYTHM STUDY NO. 3

 = c96

| 4/4 ‖: C | | F | | C | | G | |

| C | | F | | Am | | Am | :‖ C | ‖

Strum pattern:

The notated strum pattern indicates that you should play on beats 1 and 2, followed by a longer lasting strum on beat 3: 1 2 3 (4)

LISTEN AND LEARN: Rhythm Study No. 3 can be heard on CD track 3

RHYTHM STUDY NO. 4

♩ = c100

| 4/4 ‖: C | | Am | | F | | G | |

| Am | | C | | F | | F | :‖ C | ‖

Strum pattern:

The notated strum pattern indicates that you should play on beats 1, 2 and 4, with the strum on beat 2 left ringing on for two beats: 1 2 (3) 4

LISTEN AND LEARN: Rhythm Study No. 4 can be heard on CD track 4

RHYTHM STUDY ADVICE

In order to achieve the most musical performance and obtain a high mark in the exam you should aim for the following when performing the Rhythm Study:

• A secure knowledge of the chord shapes, so that you can play the chords accurately.

• The ability to change from one chord shape to another smoothly and without hesitation or delay.

• Clear sounding chords that are free of fretbuzz and any unintended muting of notes. (Pressing with the tips of the fretting fingers, as close as possible to the fretwire, will help avoid fretbuzz. This technique will also minimise the amount of fretting pressure required – enabling you to play with a lighter, and therefore more fluent, touch.)

• Accurate reproduction of the rhythm of the notated strum pattern.

• A fluent rhythm style, maintaining an even tempo throughout.

• Accurate observation of the repeat sign.

Performance

There are two options to choose from in this section of the exam, and you are free to select whichever <u>ONE</u> option you prefer.

OPTION 1

Play a melody:

You should select and perform <u>ONE</u> of the four melodies provided in this chapter.

OR

OPTION 2

Play another Rhythm Study:

If you prefer to focus on rhythm playing rather than melody playing, you can select another Rhythm Study from the previous chapter. This chord chart should then be performed either using the notated strum pattern provided with it or, if you prefer, you can use a musically appropriate rhythm of your own choosing, providing that it is of at least a similar technical standard to the notated rhythms.

If selecting this option, the chord chart that is performed must be a different one from that played in the earlier section of the exam.

If you decide to choose 'Option 2' refer to the previous Rhythm Study chapter for all the information you will require; the remainder of this chapter refers to 'Option 1' – i.e. playing a melody.

MELODY

You can select and play ONE of the four melodies notated on the following pages. You do not need to play from memory: the handbook may be used during this section of the exam. Remember to bring your handbook to the exam if you do not intend to play from memory; photocopies will not be permitted.

- The melody can be played with a pick or using fingers – it's your choice.

- The two vertical dots at the end of each melody indicate that the music should be repeated from the other set of vertical dots at the beginning – i.e. the melody should be played twice.

- Tempo markings have been chosen that reflect the capabilities expected at this level, but are for general guidance only: faster, or slightly slower, tempos can be used providing they produce an effective musical result.

- The melody must be played unaccompanied. Chord symbols are provided for each melody purely to enable a teacher or fellow player to provide accompaniment during practice. You are NOT required to play the chords in this section of the exam – only the melody, unaccompanied. (On the CD an accompaniment is provided to each melody only to enhance the musical effect and reinforce the timing for learning purposes.)

As melodies are based on scales, practising the key scale of your chosen melody will undoubtedly make learning the melody much easier, and is therefore highly recommended. All the melodies in this handbook are in the key of C major and so the fretbox and notation for the C major scale are provided below for you to practise prior to attempting to learn the melodies.

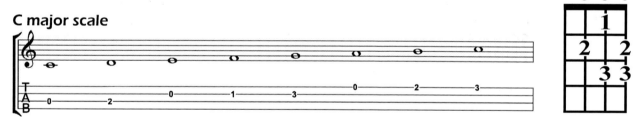

C major scale

MELODY PLAYING ADVICE

In order to achieve the most musical performance and obtain a high mark in the exam you should aim for the following when performing your chosen melody:

- An accurate reproduction of the pitch and rhythm of the melody.

- A fluent rendition, maintaining an even tempo throughout.

- Clear sounding notes that are free of fretbuzz.

- Capturing the phrasing within the melody.

- Accurate observation of the repeat markings.

WHEN THE SAINTS GO MARCHING IN

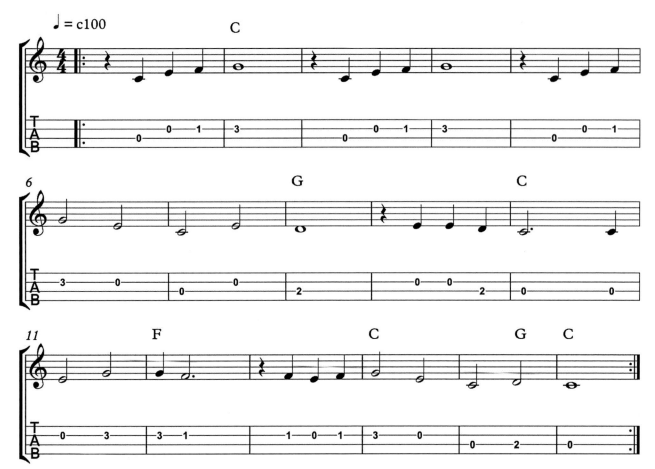

Playing Guide:

- This melody is in $^4_4$ time and the tune begins on the second beat of the bar.

- The melody is notated in the key of C major and all the notes come from the first five degrees of the C major scale.

- Notice how bars 3 and 5 are an exact repeat of bar 1.

LISTEN AND LEARN: When The Saints Go Marching In can be heard on CD track 5

14

ON TOP OF OLD SMOKEY

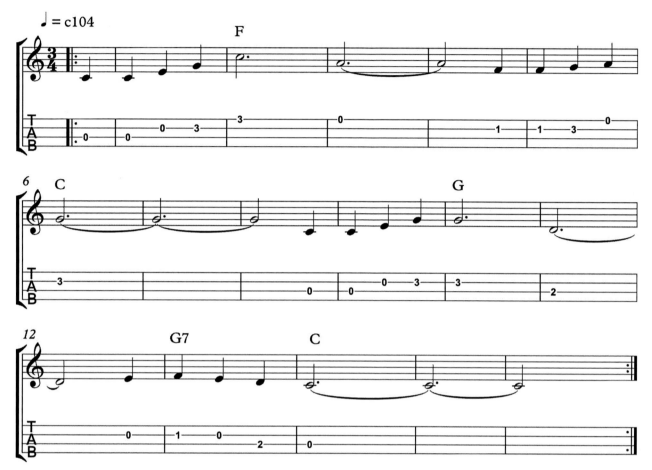

Playing Guide:

- This melody is in $\frac{3}{4}$ time and the tune begins on beat 3 (i.e. after a count of 2).

- The melody consists of four 4-bar phrases, each of which begins on the third beat of the bar and ends with a long tied note.

- The melody is notated in the key of C major and all the notes come from the C major scale.

LISTEN AND LEARN: On Top Of Old Smokey can be heard on CD track 6

MICHAEL ROW THE BOAT ASHORE

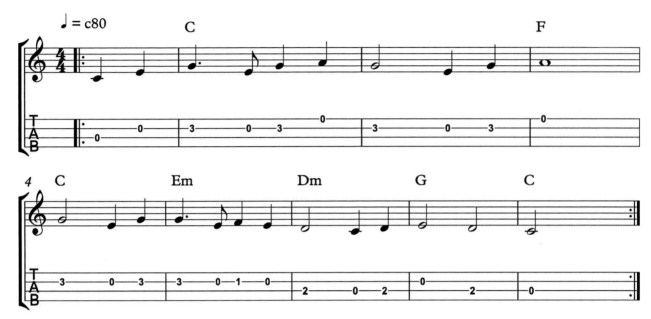

Playing Guide:

- This melody is in $\frac{4}{4}$ time. The tune begins on beat 3 (i.e. after a count of 2).

- The melody consists of two rhythmically similar phrases – the second phrase starting on beat 3 of bar 4.

- Look out for the dotted note at the start of the first full bar and bar 5, as this provides an important rhythmic feature of the melody.

- The melody is notated in the key of C major and all the notes come from the first six degrees of the C major scale.

LISTEN AND LEARN: Michael Row The Boat Ashore can be heard on CD track 7

KUMBAYA

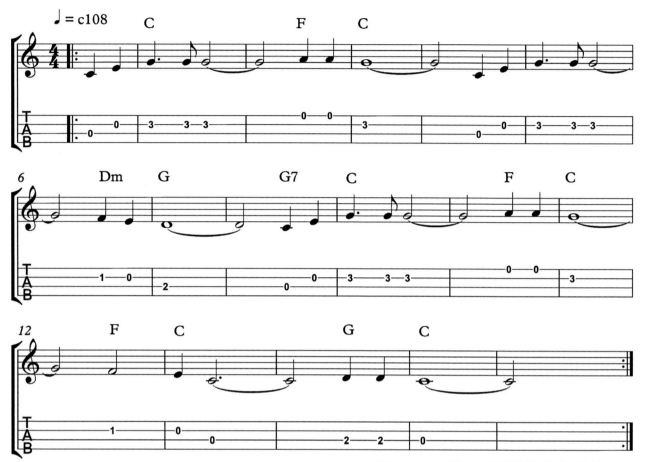

This arrangement © copyright 2014 by Registry Publications

Playing Guide:

- This melody is in $\frac{4}{4}$ time.

- The melody consists of four phrases, each of which begin halfway through a bar, on beat 3 (i.e. after a count of two). The third phrase is simply a repeat of the first.

- Several of the notes are 'tied' to make them last longer; try to allow these notes to ring for their full duration.

- The melody is notated in the key of C major and all the notes come from the first six degrees of the C major scale.

LISTEN AND LEARN: Kumbaya can be heard on CD track 8

Free Choice Specialism

There are three options to choose from in this section of the exam, and you are free to select whichever __ONE__ option you prefer.

Option 1:

You select a piece of your own choice.

The piece can be either in the format of a melody, or a solo piece, or a strummed or fingerstyle accompaniment to a song (backing tracks cannot be used). If you wish to sing whilst playing that is perfectly acceptable, but only the ukulele playing (not the singing) will be assessed.

When selecting a free choice piece, you should ensure that the chosen piece is of at least a similar technical standard and duration to the melodies or rhythm studies presented in this handbook. RGT will not advise on the suitability of free choice pieces as part of the assessment process here includes a candidate's ability to research and select an appropriate piece to perform.

OR

Option 2:

You can select and perform another melody from those provided in the Performance chapter of this handbook.

If choosing this option, the melody that is performed must be different from that played in the Performance section of the exam.

OR

Option 3:

You can select another Rhythm Study from the Rhythm Study chapter of this handbook.

This chord chart should then be performed either using the notated strum pattern provided with it or, if you prefer, you can use a musically appropriate rhythm of your own choosing, providing that it is of at least a similar technical standard to the notated rhythms.

If selecting this option, the chord chart that is performed must be different from that played in the Rhythm Study and the Performance sections of the exam.

Prepared Accompaniment

You should select <u>ONE</u> of the three tunes provided in this chapter and play an accompaniment along with it using the chord chart provided. Each tune is performed on the CD that accompanies this handbook – this enables you not only to hear how each tune sounds, but also allows you to practise your accompaniment as much as you wish with the tune in advance of the exam.

In the exam, the examiner will play your selected tune (either via a recording or live on guitar or keyboard) and you should play a suitable chordal accompaniment to this selected tune.

You do not need to play from memory; you may use your handbook during this section of the exam. Remember to bring your handbook to the exam if you do not intend to play from memory; photocopies will not be permitted.

You can choose to either strum or/and fingerpick. The style of accompaniment, including the rhythms that you use, is left to your discretion and the examiner will not advise on this. The standard of playing is expected to be equivalent to the strumming patterns shown in the Rhythm Study chapter. If you play a much simpler rhythm this will be reflected in the mark awarded.

Each tune is in $^4_4$ time and is 8 bars in length (plus a final closing bar). As on the recording, there will be a verbal one-bar count-in before the main 8-bar tune is played through once. This initial 'practice' playing is just to remind you of the tune and its timing. Another verbal one-bar count-in will then be given straightaway and the main 8-bar tune will then be played twice *without stopping*, before ending on the final closing bar note. Note that you will only be assessed during your playing in the final two verses – so you can use the first verse either just to listen or to practise (for example, by just strumming a chord once on the first beat of each bar so that you can get a feel for the timing).

The range of chords that may occur in this section of the exam is the same as those previously listed in the Rhythm Study chapter – i.e. C, F, G, Am. You can view the fretboxes for the chords in the Rhythm Study chapter. In each chord chart there are two bars of each chord, apart from the very final bar (after the repeat), in which the final chord should be played with a single strum.

You are not required to use the same fingerings for the chord shapes that are shown in this handbook – any alternative chord fingerings will be acceptable, provided the chord itself is technically accurate and musically effective.

The tunes and chord charts are shown on the following pages. The notation for the tunes is provided in this handbook primarily for situations where a teacher might wish to play the tune with a student rather than use the CD provided.

ACCOMPANIMENT NO. 1

Accompaniment Chord Chart No.1

$\left|\frac{4}{4}\right\|$: C |C |F |F |

|C |C |G |G   :|C   ‖

Accompaniment Tune No. 1   **CD Track 9**

♩ = 112

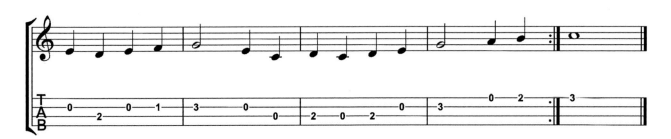

ACCOMPANIMENT NO. 2

Accompaniment Chord Chart No. 2

$\left|\frac{4}{4}\right\|$: C |C |Am |Am |

|F |F |G |G   :|C   ‖

Accompaniment Tune No. 2   **CD Track 10**

♩ = 108

ACCOMPANIMENT NO. 3

Accompaniment Chord Chart No. 3

| 4/4 :‖ Am | | Am | | F | | F | |
| C | | C | | G | | G | :‖ Am | ‖ |

Accompaniment Tune No. 3 — CD Track 11

♩ = 100

Accompaniment Advice

1. Wait until you are totally comfortable playing all the chord shapes and changing between them fluently before attempting to practise your accompaniment to the tune on the CD.

2. Remember that the first time the tune is played you have the opportunity to either listen to it without needing to play along or to practise your timing by just strumming once on the first beat of each bar.

3. In the remaining two verses use an appropriate rhythm that suits the timing and style of the tune.

4. Keep listening closely to the tune while playing your accompaniment and make sure to keep in time with it. Try to ensure that your chord changes come in clearly on the first beat of each bar, to help establish a definite pulse and rhythm.

5. Pay attention to how the chords sound and check that the fretting fingers are pressing with their tips and are as close to the frets as possible in order to ensure that all the strings are ringing out clearly, without fretbuzz or unintended muted notes.

6. If you make a mistake, avoid the temptation to stop. It is essential that you keep playing so that you do not lose your place in the music and fall out of time with the tune. Regardless of what mistake you might make with a chord shape, it will never be as damaging to the performance as if you come to a complete stop – particularly as the tune will carry on without you. If you cannot change to a chord in time, try placing your fretting hand across the strings to mute them whilst you carry on strumming until you can find your place in the music again – it's not ideal, but it will definitely sound preferable to a total halt and the risk of losing your co-ordination with the tune.

Musicianship

The examiner will conduct a short selection of aural awareness tests. At this level the tests are restricted to the examiner playing two notes, one after the other, and, without using your instrument, you will be asked to state whether the second note was higher or lower than the first note. The interval between the two notes will be a perfect 4th or larger, but no more than an octave. The tests may be played by the examiner on guitar or piano, or via a recording.

In the exam, four tests will be given: two where the second note is higher than the first note and two where it is lower. Each test will only be played once and you should try to give your answer promptly and confidently after hearing the notes.

Below are some *examples* of the type of tests that will be given.

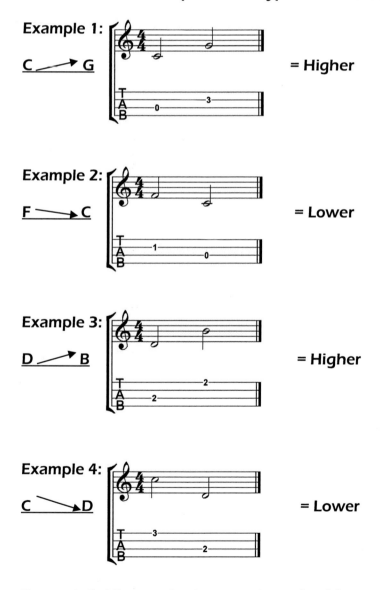

Example 1:

C ➝ G   = Higher

Example 2:

F ➝ C   = Lower

Example 3:

D ➝ B   = Higher

Example 4:

C ➝ D   = Lower

Please note that the examples above are only samples of the type of tests that will be given in the exam.

Registry of Guitar Tutors

Exam Entry Form
Ukulele Initial Stage

ONLINE ENTRY – AVAILABLE FOR UK CANDIDATES ONLY

For **UK candidates**, entries and payments can be made online at www.RGT.org, using the entry code below. You will be able to pay the entry fee by credit or debit card at a secure payment page on the website.

Your unique and confidential exam entry code is:

UN-1836-AQ

Keep this unique code confidential, as it can only be used once. Once you have entered online, you should sign this form overleaf. **You must bring this signed form to your exam and hand it to the examiner in order to be admitted to the exam room.**

If NOT entering online, please complete BOTH sides of this form and return to the address overleaf.

SESSION (Spring/Summer/Winter): _____ YEAR: _____

Dates/times NOT available: _____

Note: Only name *specific* dates (and times on those dates) when it would be <u>absolutely impossible</u> for you to attend due to important prior commitments (such as pre-booked overseas travel) which cannot be cancelled. We will then endeavour to avoid scheduling an exam session in your area on those dates. In fairness to all other candidates in your area, **only list dates on which it would be impossible for you to attend.** An entry form that blocks out unreasonable periods may be returned. (Exams may be held on any day of the week including, but not exclusively, weekends. Exams may be held within or outside of the school term.)

Candidate Details: *Please write as clearly as possible using BLOCK CAPITALS*

Candidate Name (as to appear on certificate): _____

Address: _____

_____ Postcode: _____

Tel. No. (day): _____ (mobile): _____

IMPORTANT: Take care to write your email address below as clearly as possible, as your exam entry acknowledgement and your exam appointment details will be sent to this email address. Only provide an email address that is in regular monitored use.

Email:_____

Where an email address is provided your exam correspondence will be sent by email only, and not by post. This will ensure your exam correspondence will reach you sooner.

Teacher Details *(if applicable)*

Teacher Name (as to appear on certificate): _____

RGT Tutor Code (if applicable):_____

Address: _____

_____ Postcode: _____

Tel. No. (day): _____ (mobile): _____

Email:_____

RGT Ukulele Official Entry Form

The standard LCM entry form is NOT valid for RGT exam entries.

Entry to the exam is only possible via this original form.

Photocopies of this form will not be accepted under any circumstances.

- Completion of this entry form is an agreement to comply with the current syllabus requirements and conditions of entry published at www.RGT.org. Where candidates are entered for exams by a teacher, parent or guardian that person hereby takes responsibility that the candidate is entered in accordance with the current syllabus requirements and conditions of entry.

- If you are being taught by an *RGT registered* tutor, please hand this completed form to your tutor and request him/her to administer the entry on your behalf.

- For candidates with special needs, a letter giving details should be attached.

Exam Fee: £_____   Late Entry Fee (if applicable): £_____

Total amount submitted: £_____

Cheques or postal orders should be made payable to Registry of Guitar Tutors.

Details of conditions of entry, entry deadlines and exam fees are obtainable from the RGT website: www.RGT.org

Once an entry has been accepted, entry fees cannot be refunded.

CANDIDATE INFORMATION (UK Candidates only)

In order to meet our obligations in monitoring the implementation of equal opportunities policies, UK candidates are required to supply the information requested below. The information provided will in no way whatsoever influence the marks awarded during the exam.

Date of birth: _____   Age: _____   Gender – please circle: male / female

Ethnicity (please enter 2 digit code from chart below): _____   Signed: _____

ETHNIC ORIGIN CLASSIFICATIONS (If you prefer not to say, write '17' in the space above.)

White: **01 British**   **02 Irish**   **03 Other white background**

Mixed: **04 White & black Caribbean**   **05 White & black African**   **06 White & Asian**   **07 Other mixed background**

Asian or Asian British: **08 Indian**   **09 Pakistani**   **10 Bangladeshi**   **11 Other Asian background**

Black or Black British: **12 Caribbean**   **13 African**   **14 Other black background**

Chinese or Other Ethnic Group: **15 Chinese**   **16 Other**   **17 Prefer not to say**

I understand and accept the current syllabus regulations and conditions of entry for this exam as specified on the RGT website.

Signed by candidate (if aged 18 or over) _____   Date _____

If candidate is under 18, this form should be signed by a parent/guardian/teacher (circle which applies):

Signed _____   Name_____   Date_____

UK ENTRIES

See overleaf for details of how to enter online OR return this form to:

Registry of Guitar Tutors, Registry Mews, 11 to 13 Wilton Road, Bexhill-on-Sea, E. Sussex, TN40 1HY
(If you have submitted your entry online do NOT post this form, instead you need to sign it above and hand it to the examiner on the day of your exam.)
To contact the RGT office telephone 01424 222222 or Email office@RGT.org

NON-UK ENTRIES

To locate the address within your country that entry forms should be sent to, and to view exam fees in your currency, visit the RGT website **www.RGT.org** and navigate to the 'RGT Worldwide' section.